TAKE THIS BOOK AS YOU WILL

PHILLIP MAGAÑA

To the misfists of the world...

Do You, Be You

Storytime: Nevermore

There was a man who lived by the Sun, but loved by Luna. He would get sad by the waxing and waning of her, and Luna, who shined above in the night, would notice his tears.

Luna would ask, "Why do you cry for me?"

The man answered, "You've always been with me, and there are times when the people here on Earth, who are supposed to be closest to me, seem as far away from me as the distance between us."

Luna spoke: "I'll always be with you, no matter what happens in your life. Take comfort in knowing I'll be with you until the end of your days."

And that was good enough for the man, for through the years, as she waxed and waned through the night sky, Luna was there with him. He took comfort knowing that she was there, through all stages of his life.

When the man became old and his journey was at its end, he received a special visitor at his bedside: it was Luna's aspect. He smiled brightly at her like the Sun, overjoyed by her presence.

"You had a good yet lonely life", Luna said. "I'm sorry you never found true love."

"But I did," he smiled. "I found it in you." The man rose from his bed to his feet, embracing Luna, who smiled and shed a tear.

"Why the tears, dear Luna?"

"Because everyone needs love, and you gave that to me. Thank you."

And with a kiss, they scintillate like a sparkler into the night, to leave each other's side...nevermore.

Comfort and Contempt

This is life, right?

It's where you miss opportunities, make mistakes, and learn valuable lessons, correct?

It's a series of events where you hope to make good on the time you have, form a tribe, and maybe fall in love?

Somewhere along the way, all that skipped me.

Sometimes it feels like Life is having me live outside the box to learn different lessons than everyone else.

Sometimes it feels like Life is playing a dirty joke on me, where only it gets the punchline.

Maybe I see it, maybe I've just ignored it.

The punchline is probably where I live outside the box, while wandering inside the box of my living room, watching everyone else live life and do them.

Maybe the punchline is where everyone doesn't want me to leave this comfortable spot so they know where I'm at, at all times, just so it makes them feel better about themselves.

That's it then. That's the punchline.

I'm supposed to waste away in comfortability just like them...

Fault

You always ask your heart for help yet always deny its advice

You want your heart to guide you yet don't follow its lead when it shows the way

All that, yet you have the nerve to complain when it abandons you

-pm-

Real Magic

There are days when a kiss and a smile make past
bullshit disappear.

When a hug's energy heals hidden wounds and
revives the soul.

How about when a simple "I love you" makes you
forget bad happenings?

That's Magic. That's Real.

-pm-

Us and That

It isn't the love you give, but it's a bonus.

It's not your smile that warms my heart, but I appreciate that.

Could it be the kisses you slip in throughout the day when we're together? Naw, but those make me feel good.

It's you. Your style, your charm.

When you bring it in for a hug.

When we laugh like kids and do our thing.

It's you.

You.

-pm-

Strength

I found out the hard way, like many people do, that strength isn't built in a gym pushing weight.

It's surviving your hardships, your struggles. It's looking in the mirror, smiling at yourself, knowing you did it.

-pm-

Lesson

Pain is part of Life's game.
Own it, learn from it,
but never let it consume you.

-pm-

Don't/Quit

Girl...

Quit trying to change me
I'm not a dog you can train
I'm not someone you can mold
like clay to show off to your friends

I met you as a complete person
Don't treat me simple,
don't treat me as a compliment
Love me like you did,
before your friends tried to dictate

A little Tough Love

Everyone goes through heartbreak.
Get over it.
Take it as a lesson that the Universe
sent you:
Nothing in Life is easy.

-pm-

Storytime: Video Game

I do my life as a video game...

I know certain moves to help
me win, not to help anyone else win.

You have to figure out those moves on your own. All I
know is how to beat the boss level my way, how to get
past certain trails, certain paths, done my way.

Be the start of your own video game, do the moves to
help YOU win.

In the end, that's all that matters

Peace.

-pm-

Unpredictable

Hot damn. Love is being unpredictable again!

Just when you think everything's cool,
along comes someone who makes your
heart race.

-pm-

Feelin' You

Looking in your eyes,
I see hope,
a chance.
Something that was missing
from my life.

-pm-

Midnight Sun

You with your whiskey,
me with the tequila.
A summer's evening,
chillin' by the fire pit.
We give that look,
our shirts come off.
We step close,
the magic happens.

In the distance,
we hear the wolves howl.

-pm-

Selfish

Imma be selfish...
I wasn't ready for you to go yet.

Wasn't ready for the empty void I
knew was coming.
You told me as a kid, "nothing lasts".

You told me as a man, "protect this house".
You told me in a dream, *"sangre espesa"*.

I'd trade all those lessons for one
more day, Grandma.
I had so many questions and
more things to learn.

I should've paid attention more.
What's up with the *Pinche Triste* feelings?

I just miss you.

-pm-

Gravity

It starts with a smile.

The kind that makes you
smile back and warms hearts.

The one that makes you get
past your shyness and makes
you do something you rarely do.

That lets you approach that
person and say hi, 'cause their
smile has that kind of gravity.

-pm-

Christina

Leave it to one person who loved us
all to reunite old friends and family.

A smile for everyone,
a mischievous nature,
and a heart that ran wild!

Thank you for bringing us together again,
but you should be here with us laughing,
cussing and carrying on.

You said don't cry for you,
but we can't help it.
It's what you do when
family goes away.

You said, we'll see each other again someday,
maybe I won't.

I did things I can't be forgiven for,
and we'll have to wave
at each other from
opposite sides of the
gate on that day.

Don't worry. As we
said long ago...

Amigos por siempre!

-pm-

Love You

Light, Dark, doesn't matter.
Let her be your Sword
against the bad things...

She wears you as her Armor
against the Storm

-pm-

Closed

Live, dammit!

You can't live a full life being closed up!

Share this life, you won't be sorry.

-pm-

Grateful

Grateful for my life
Love those who have helped me grow
Blessings to my tribe

-pm-

4.29.18

There's love behind that smile.

See that sparkle in your eye?

See how that nose wrinkles up as your eyes and cheeks pinch it together?

Feel that warmth as you look at your close ones, and it radiates to them?

See how that smile gives comfort to others?

There's love behind that smile.

-pm-

Not Perfect

I'm not trying to
find the perfect woman.

I'd love a woman
who'd give me
a genuine smile
and return my calls.

And drinking shots
of tequila off of
Schultz Pass Road
wouldn't hurt, either.

-pm-

Mami

When she's next to me, a mischievous smile on me...

When her fingers search my body for that sweet spot...

Her warm kisses on my lips, teasing me to smile...

Arms and legs entwined, threatening to never let go...

The heat, the energy when we're close...

Was it ever supposed to feel like this?

Hell no. It's better.

-pm-

Storytime: Blame Game

There was a time I blamed my troubles on everyone else. I pointed my finger at everyone, everything.

Women were my worst enemy, especially my mama.

"I did no wrong," I thought. "I do all the right moves, I do all the right things."

But still, all my bads were blamed on other people.

Then one day, after not having my so-called enemies to blame anymore, I looked in the mirror.

I saw myself.

The worst enemy of all.

I wanted to blame someone for my pain, for the bad going on in my life.

I pointed the finger at that sumbitch in the mirror.

On that day, and since then, I only have myself to blame for the wrongs to myself, and started taking baby steps to put things right.

Eventually, we all run out of enemies to blame.

The biggest enemy is within ourselves.

When you see your Enemy Within, on that day, I hope you get right with yourself.

-pm-

Haiku

And so, the day came,
the day I crushed my own heart,
when I said goodbye.

-pm-

Haiku

A full moon howling,
celebrated with a shot,
I take one for you.

-pm-

Slow Love

Time slows with you

Maybe my perceptions do that since
I want to savor our moments

When you're around, love's everlasting

The hugs are deep and long

The kisses leave me breathless

We won't start on the butterflies, since they don't stop
when you're not around

What I do know, is I don't want this feeling to ever end

-pm-

Stagnant

Stagnant people are the ones
who help fuel dreams

When you join that pack,
you've killed your dreams.

-pm-

Word

When you think about it, you don't know what life has in store for your ass.

The daily motion and grind. The struggles, laughter and tears. The moments of happiness mixed with your favorite shots.

Oh, you don't drink? Good for you. Might help you cope with other people's bullshit.

Now, I ain't mad atcha. To each their own but don't judge other people's grind. Their flow, their d-lo.

So, cheers to Life, baby! You made it this far. Be proud, be bold, be brave.

A ramble poem? Damn right. Got hella love for my tribe. You, the one reading this.

One Love.

Peace.

-pm-

Storytime: Peace Be Your Journey

Some people will fall from you on your journey.
Things happen, that's just Life. You have every right to
protect yourself, you have a right to cut people off who
treat you like an afterthought after you treat them with
love.

You have this One Life to make it right. That means
you don't have to put up with bullshit that you know
you have control over, and that's your time,
 space,
energy.
Don't devalue yourself by trying to show someone
who couldn't care less about you, you're good people.
If you're doing all that, it means they're not good
people to begin with. Cut them the fuck loose and
move on with your Journey.

It will be lonely, your Journey, the more you walk
alone. Good quality people will come into your life as
you drop the shit baggage from your life, remember
that.

Those are the ones that know your worth, and will
truly help you remember it.

Peace.

This Moment

I never thought I'd make it this far...

All the shit I've done in my life like the drinking, smoking, partying, crazy adventures...

Buck Wildin' at too early an age has left me feeling I've nothing left to accomplish...

Being a "good son" has me feeling broken and unmotivated...

The single dad life left me alone and occasionally heartbroken...

Marriage and Divorce? Don't get me started on that bullshit!

Old aches and pains and damage leaves me feeling, well, more damaged than I actually am...

Then I remember something, a feeling...

It hits like a good pull from some old school Chronic joint...

I hate boredom. I despise it...

When the call of adventure rings out...when it whispers daily in my ear like a long-lost lover...

When I feel that pull, everything comes alive again!

And I remember, I'm build for it, this life, with all its heartache and pain, joys and sorrows...

All the adventures it's blessed me with, all the people who I've met and are part of my life...

I remember the journey and what it means to me...

To be joyous, to be free, to be me!

A Little Love

Poems.

   I don't write them to get famous.

I write them for therapy.

   And maybe,

along the way,

   they help someone

who could use a

   little TLC themselves.

Crazy

It's my biggest hope
that the person reading this
will release their true power
and be the crazy bastard
   the crazy loving
      the crazy living
         the crazy adventurous fucker
they always see staring
   back at them from reflections

As A Man

You're a man

   You're a warrior
   You're not perfect
   Don't pretend to be

As a man

   You're the first line of defense
   For your friends
   For your family
   For your children

Yes, you will take a beating in life

   From the doubters, the naysayers
   Stand strong, stand firm
   Build that armor against the world

You're gonna need it

Everyone will try to rewrite what a man is

In your heart, you already know

We are kindness
We are strength
We are love

Don't forget that

As the world tries to rewrite us

Hope

Looking in your eyes,
I see hope,
a chance.
Something that was missing from
my life.

Sweeter

The day I met you,
I knew that life's adventures
would be much sweeter.

Touch

Sad to say,
but you can't save everyone.

Sometimes,
you have to let Life's hard caress
teach them the truth.

Got You

Remember the time that slow jam was bumping from a car when we were walking down the street, we stopped, and we slow-danced on the sidewalk?

Remember the time when you were in a bad mood, I stole a kiss anyway, and you still smiled?

Remember the time when you needed a hug, and I was filthy from work, and you still hugged me in that pretty blue number you wore?

Remember the time we went to bed mad at each other, backs facing each other, but we still held hands?

Remember the time we watched the sunset after you lost a friend, and I said "I got you"?

Always remember that.

No matter what...

I got you.

Again

I did it again.

Played in the garden of Eden when I shouldn't have.

Now I'm wandering again, alone, like I deserve.

I did it again.

Lonesome

His lonesome eyes
saw past that
bullshit exterior
and saw you
that woman
ready to fuck the
world up with her
own brand
of love

Yet

Strong yet vulnerable
Brave yet broken

Yet he moved forward...

Someday

It sucks when your heart aches
for something it had a taste of,
then gets yanked away.

Then you remember...

You'll have that taste
again someday.
But it won't be a taste,
it'll be for real.

-pm-

Please

Babygirl...

Someday you'll understand
why I love you so hard...

And someday,
I'll understand why you
keep me at arm's length
because of his mistakes...

Package Deal

heartbreak

our greatest
lesson
pain
strength

all in one nice package

9.11.18

those days you want to disappear in the crowd but you know you're not built like that...

sleepless nights when you feel so damn lonely but you feel Nature's Caress pulling you outside to wrap her evening blanket around you for comfort...

remembering those times when you had that love to share yet yanked from you and now finding strength in standing alone...

those Arizona sunsets you shared and watching the sun dip until you couldn't stare anymore, then you watched a different sunset in each other's eyes...

and yet it still wasn't enough...

no, I had to taste you more in different ways...

those kisses...

that deep, slow grind...

those hugs we couldn't pull apart from...

damn girl, thank you for giving me love...

Mmm, that's how I remember it.

That's what love is.

Me

Somewhere along the way,
we stop listening to our hearts.
Other people's opinions matter,
their words carry weight,
and a heart gets drowned out
among the bullshit.

Somewhere along the way,
when you decide to stand up
for yourself and tell everyone
that your heart matters
and not them,
you make enemies.
The people who were there
for you before, won't be.

Somewhere along the way,
when you're standing alone
after the dust settles of
standing up for yourself
and listening to your heart,
those who understand,
those who feel the way you do,
fill in the holes of those left behind.

They fill it with love, understanding, patience. They've given you what you sought this whole time...

A family of understanding.

And it's all good.

Hard

Babygirl...

Saying goodbye is never the hard part,
being friends isn't the hard part,
being cool with each other after so
much
love between us
isn't the hard part.

It's seeing you alone out there,
wanting to run up to you
and giving you a hug and kiss
like I used to,
but not being able to,

That's the hard part.

Gamble

You think you've figured me out, don't you?

Think you know how my heart beats, am I right?

Oh, you say you know how I'll react to the way you
hold my hand to feel the butterflies?

And you think you'll see me smile when you tell me
you're in for the long haul because I deserve love?

Damn, this would be money well lost.

Feels Good

Music,
my medicine

Dance,
my therapy

Writing,
my release

Life,
my reward

Please

Babygirl...

Hold my hand for a bit.
I need your strength, your love.
It's there, I just need to feel it.

I need to know, through my own
bad thoughts and doubts,
you won't abandon me
like the last one.

Storytime: In my own footsteps

I walk this journey alone.

Through its ups, downs, twists and turns, I've tried to remain steadfast on my journey, not the destination.

Through all this, I've had beautiful people join me along the way. Many started off with me, many departed, very few continue along with me.

Someday, there will be that one who will walk with me to the very end.

I'm looking forward to that.

In the meantime, I continue this journey alone with the shining lights above me. My tribe. My lights in this crazy Darkness, but I've never been afraid of the dark. I've learned to embrace it.

I stand fast in the Darkness, helping my tribe along the way while they shine brightly. We each have a role to play. Yin and Yang.

But I'll continue to walk alone.

This is my journey.

And it's my strength.

Challenge

I hate stagnation,
I always crave a challenge.
I push my limits.

Hate

There's no room for hate.
Save that shit for yourself, man.
You seem to like it.

Worth It

There was a time when love was all. When love was worth fighting for, worth dying for.

I remember loving all the wrong people, and when the smoke cleared from my heart, I was fucking jaded.

Blame youth, blame the wrong head, blame the competition...naw, I blame me for being fucking stupid.

I was a sucker for girls, and they knew it. Some preyed on it. You know, damsel in distress to get their wish.

Time passed. I wised up. Listened to my sisters and lady friends when they schooled me about females.

That's not what I needed schooling in. Love was the problem. I didn't want to catch feelings too fast.

I didn't want to be love-struck after one conversation like some junior high kid after that first kiss.

Then I learned something about love...do so with all your heart. Do it with your heart on your sleeve.

Why? I asked myself. Why put myself through that kind of pain, that hurt? Didn't I learn the first few times?

The answer came through more heartache. Because this is LIFE, plain and simple.

You give your all, you don't half-ass it. You can't run from it. You take the sweet with the sour.

So, I learned from all that madness, that love is worth it. You can't run from it, because it's all around.

I embraced it. Not for anyone else. Not because it's expected of me...

Because I want to live, fully and totally. No restrictions.

Because it's worth it.

Regrets

Babygirl...

You asked me why I wear my heart on
my sleeve, when it leaves me wide open.

One of us has to be fully committed,
and I want no regrets if I walk away

Moments

Babygirl...

I know I go slow.
The kisses, the love making,
our walks, our talks

I know I go slow,
because I'm making
our moments last

Bring it in

Babygirl...

Bring it in for a hug
I see the weariness in your eyes,
feel your tired energy
Let me share mine

Bring it in for one
You've been my rock plenty
Time for me to be yours

Smile for Me

Babygirl...

You got that smile again
That one where you're comfortable
with yourself and dropped dead
friendships that weren't loving

Because you love me and I haven't
abandoned you, you say?
I ain't going nowhere and love you more.
Now, smile for me?

Story Past

I'm tired of being alone while everyone
walks with someone...

How much longer do I have to get good, before
someone realizes I'm good?

I see people together who don't belong that way,
at least they have someone, right?

I was the "god guy" folks depended on,
but where has it gotten me?

Still alone, sometimes sad, many times angry,
then one day, I said, "I'll be bad!"

Man, girls noticed me then. They flocked to me,
sex was satisfied, it fulfilled my needs.

Being an asshole was paying off, it got me a raise, and
still, girls were flocking!

One day, as I rolled over and looked that this girl, this
stranger lying comfortably in my bed,

I came to a fucked-up truth...

She's still getting dressed and leaving.

Still going home while I have breakfast alone,
but at least my bed smells good!

Still gonna have dinner alone,
making too much leftovers,
but at least I'll have that for days!

For days, but still alone. Still wanting and chasing,
while others find compliments, not completeness.

One day, I chased them all away!

One day, I decided to get good with me,
to stop being half-assed!

Why? Because the loneliness was still there,
but it was fun while it lasted.

Girls don't cure shit, only I knew deep down,
I had to be my own cure.

So, I was nice again, 'cause that was me, but it was
hard.

Tasting the Wild Side was fuckin' orgasmic,
it made me at ease.

And that was the goddamn key, right?
To find that balance inside.

To find my self-worth while others questioned,
and find strength in their doubting.

I still walk alone, it's all good with me,
I still praise those who found their Complete.

Someday I know,
and without expecting it,
I'll get blindsided by Cupid's punk ass arrow!

I'll walk by her side, and she by mine,
and the catch I know will happen...

I'll already be complete.

Journey On

I used to be scared of Life.

Scared of her Lessons,
Scared of her Demands,
Scared of her Drama.

I couldn't hang what was
being thrown at me,
what was being taken from me.

Then one day it clicked.

Life is full of surprises,
Life is easy for no one,
Life is to have adventures.

Life taught me to take the hand
I've been dealt and win the best I can.

But a lesson I taught myself,
you don't have to accept what is.

If you have the courage,
you have the power to change it!

Life also taught me the best lesson ever...

She's worth living,
but it's a choice I have to make.

And her journey is well worth the Destination.

Maybe, Someday

Your touch, your lips,
your smell, your kiss.
My mind said no,
but my heart said yes

This crazy love we have,
we know it's wrong.
You belong to someone else,
but I know you belong with me.

We should care,
but we don't.
We can't deny each other,
we know the heartache is there.

Maybe, someday,
when we go through
that heartbreak that
will happen,
we'll be together.

Time

Somewhere...

In another time,
In another place,
In another lifetime...

We're together.

We're Home.

How I wish that somewhere, were now.

A Stone Heart

My streetwise homegirl
schooled me one day...

"There's a special strength in a man's vulnerability.

It takes an enormous amount of trust to open up to
someone like that

Whenever a man can feel comfortable enough to
express his true romantic side, it should be cherished
and celebrated."

Then she dropped
knowledge to the wise...

"Want to lose that trust?
Betray his vulnerability."

-pm-

Muerta

Death is the final countdown that inspires me.

Yeah, she's that woman in our lives that's constant,
that's always smiling at us.

She waits for us with bated breath every second of our
lives, hoping to embrace us lovingly

Death, you're a bad bitch. Many of us realize you're
our ultimate prize that we take for granted

You've made me grow, you know that?

Made me realize I have shit to do before I meet you,
for that kiss that's gonna be oh so juicy, the kind I like!

Don't worry, I'll make sure to have stories to tell you
when my time is done

But you already know that, Muerta.

Wish

I wish I could take away the pain and heartache you've endured over the years loving the wrong person...

But if I did that, you wouldn't have the strength you have now...

12.26.18

I've never been that damn naive to believe I don't live
without regret

I've done shit I'll always wish I could take back, things
I wish didn't happen when I knew damn well what
was happening.

Lessons, right?

Regrets keep me going, regrets keep me from
repeating stupid shit.

I embrace my bullshit, especially that quiet mistress
called regret.

I'd be a fool not to.

This is Us

Babygirl...

I'm a Ride or Die guy.

I want a life partnership.

No expectations, just love,
communication, and joy.

There's too much shit
that comes with marriage.

We define what togetherness is.

Dream

I love you like I do...

	You're my dream come true.

-pm-

First Kiss

I will smile for you,
if you let me kiss you first.
We'll both be happy.

Tease

I am your soulmate.
Your soul blows kisses to mine.
I think she's a tease.

Bliss

This sexual bliss,
we feel so good together.
Sunrise makes us chill.

Cricket

Mysterious eve
A little cricket dances
despite the sugar

Grow

Give someone
  the love they're missing
in their life
  and watch them grow
into the person they're meant to be.

Remember

Remember...

If someone thinks you're fake, they're describing themselves.

If someone comes at you half-ass, they're a half-ass person.

If someone bitches and complains too much, they're showing their unhappiness with themselves.

If someone trash talks others, they trash talk you.

If someone always has the answers, they really know nothing.

And if you continue to be around these people, then you deserve what you get.

-pm-

Shine

Babygirl...

Handling things like a boss is getting
you nowhere...

instead, handle it like a queen, and
watch how fast you shine!

-pm-

What I've Learned

(My Life Quotes)

Do one thing for
yourself every day.

That's not selfish,
that's self-maintenance.

Set Goals.
Be Grateful.
Work Hard.
Play Fucking Harder.

**All reunions
aren't good.
There's a reason
people stop
being friends.
Energy and
priorities change.**

You can spend your
lifetime fighting or
learning.

Use the one that will
benefit your life the
most.

It's okay to be lost, mijo.
Just don't disappear.

-Grandma Vivian

Storytime: One Thing

When my time comes, I want to know I gave it my all.
Through all the good, bad, crazy times, I want to know
deep in my soul I fought for damn near everything in
my life. Whether it was for love, respect, for my life, or
friendships, I fought for the things that matter to me
the most.

When my time comes, I want all those who I love the
most to know I'll miss them. It's supposed to be the
other way around, right? In the Summerland, you can
still feel, experience, and love those still in their mortal
shells. I'll be jealous as fuck, they'll still be able to have
ice cream and tamales, dammit! I'll miss having all that
with them. I'll miss their smiles, laughter, talks, cries,
hopes and dreams.

Most of all, when my times comes, I'll miss my son.
Being a single dad is the greatest achievement any man
can have. We raise kids into adults and hope we did
right by them. We hope they'll continue to grow into
their own being and pass on whatever lessons they've
learned to their kids. For me, my son saved me, in
more ways than I can list here.

What's the one thing I want most of all when my time
comes?

For everyone to realize that we need to work together.
We share this world and shouldn't be separated by
class, race, religion, or all that other petty bullshit.
Working together, we can achieve our full potential in
love, unity, and as a species.

One can hope, right?

Peace.

1.5.19

Storytime: Different

I always knew I was different from other people.

I'm a loner, for starters. Always did shit alone, always had a thirst for knowledge and learning. Growing up, it intensified. I got curious about everything and wanted to learn everything I could in life.

As I grew older, folks wanted to rule my life, determine what was good for me instead of asking what I wanted to do. I fought against their bullshit for a long time. What did I want to do?

I wanted to be a writer. An adventurer. Someone who could help others fulfill their dreams because there were people out there who would try to fuck their dreams up. Who were these people, you ask?

Family.

I was never told I could be whatever I wanted to be. I was always told get a job with benefits, fuck your dreams, work hard, and worry about having fun when you retire. I didn't want that, but it worked.

For years, I complied. Not because I wanted to, but I got tired of hearing the same bullshit spout at me for years. I got tired of fighting the very people who were supposed to love and encourage me. Remember, I said SUPPOSED.

During those years, I worked odd and end jobs. I still wrote, but mostly to satisfy my creative mind side. Also, I got married a few times and had a son from my first wife. It was during his birth that I knew I had a choice to make: follow my heart or follow the sheep.

It was a long, hard road, but I decided to follow my heart. It was a decision that wasn't popular with my immediate fam, but I fought back. I knew my son had to have a chance in this world, so I went back to college at the request of my dad, who had cancer. Did the damn thing for 4 years and finally graduated with my AA from the community college.

It's a lesson I wanted to show my son: finish what you started.

So, here's the lesson: finish what you started. I started off as a kid wanting to tell stories, I'm going to my grave telling stories. Folks will float from one job to another, trying to find what "sings" to them, and I hope they find it. Writing sings to me, being a storyteller sings to me, helping others sings to me. Why not be in a medium where I can do all three?

Dare to be different and find what sings to you.

Do you, be you.

Peace.

9.8.18

C+ Studios Presents:

Take This Book As You Will
By Phillip Magaña

Edited by D.L. Mendoza

Phillip Magaña, aka Me, can be reached
at the following social media outlets:

Instagram: @phillipmagana
Facebook: PhillipMaganaWrites
Tumbler: phillipmagana
Twitter: @PhilMagana

Guess what?

My halfbreed ass will return...

I still don't take good pics, but right now, I'm riding Life for all it's worth. We all should.